U.S. Military Boxing Manual

U.S. Military Boxing Manual

U.S. Military Boxing Manual

U.S. Military Boxing Manual

ISBN: 978-0-9910285-6-6

Author(s): Kambiz Mostofizadeh, U.S. Military

Publisher: Mikazuki Publishing House

Date Published: January 1st, 2015

Description: The U.S. Military Boxing Manual is an

official manual used at the United States Military

Academy in West Point, New York.

Whether you are an amateur or professional, this is

a must have for the boxing enthusiast.

Mikazuki Publishing House believes that education

is the key to happiness.

U.S. Military Boxing Manual

TABLE OF CONTENTS

U.S. Military Boxing Manual

History of Boxing

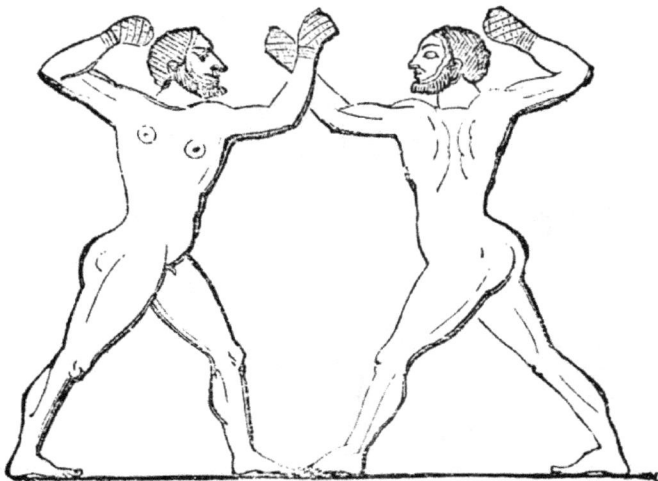

Boxing dates back to 4000 B.C.E. and

was practiced by Sumerians, Egyptians,

Greeks and Romans as a form of

entertainment. Boxing did not however enter

the Olympics until the 7th century B.C.E.

Boxers used soft leather wraps around their

hands and forearms to protect themselves.

Romans began to use the 'cestus' as a boxing

U.S. Military Boxing Manual

glove. The 'cestus' was a padded glove

studded with metal.

It was not until 17th and 18th century

England, that amateur boxing became very

popular. The first documented fight was in

1681 and in 1719 James Figg was announced

as the English bare knuckle Boxing champion.

James Figg had almost 300 fights and he won

every single one of them. John 'Jack'

Broughton, one of Figg's students, became the

U.S. Military Boxing Manual

Bare Knuckle Boxing Champion from 1729-

1750. Broughton is widely hailed as the 'Father

of English Boxing'. Daniel Mendoza, Boxing

Champion from 1791-1795 introduced

footwork, sparring, and counter punching to the

sport of Boxing. At the end of the 18th century,

William Futrell who was at one time an English

boxing champion published the first newspaper

dedicated to boxing. In 1838, London Prize

Fighting Rules were implemented that made

illegal biting, headbutting, and hitting below the

belt. These rules also set the standard for a

boxing ring at 24 feet (7.3 meters). The rules

also stipulated a boxer had to stand up from a

knockdown in less than 30 seconds for it to not

be ruled a knockout. On Feb 7, 1849, the first

American boxing championship took place with

U.S. Military Boxing Manual

Tom Hyer emerging victorious over "Yankee"
Sullivan in 16 rounds. In 1867, the Marquess of
Queensberry Rules (written by Arthur Graham
Chambers) were introduced that added to the
sport of Boxing the three minute rounds with
one minute rest time in between rounds. The
Queensberry Rules also made obligatory the
boxing glove, introduced the ten second
knockdown, outlawed holding, outlawed biting,
outlawed tripping, outlawed hitting the back of
the head, and outlawed hitting the kidneys.
John Sullivan became Bare Knuckle
Heavyweight Champion in 1882, rising to
prominence in international notoriety. In 1892,
"Gentleman" Jim Corbett became the first
Heavyweight Boxing Champion under the
"Queensberry Rules" by defeating John

U.S. Military Boxing Manual

Sullivan in New Orleans. This event highlighted the superiority of technical boxing skills and footwork in contrast to brute strength.

MANEUVER

Maneuver - /məˈnuːvər/ [N.] A maneuver is any skillful piece of management by which we accomplish our own intentions and frustrate those of our antagonist. From the Old French word 'manovre' meaning handwork and manual labor.

U.S. Military Boxing Manual

MARQUESS OF QUEENSBERRY RULES

(1867)

1. To be a fair stand-up boxing match in a 24-foot ring, or as near that size as practicable.

2. No wrestling or hugging allowed.

U.S. Military Boxing Manual

3. The rounds to be of three minutes' duration, and one minute's time between rounds.

4. If either man falls through weakness or otherwise, he must get up unassisted, 10 seconds to be allowed him to do so, the other man meanwhile to return to his corner, and when the fallen man is on his legs the round is to be resumed and continued until the three minutes have expired. If one man fails to come to the scratch in the 10 seconds allowed, it shall be in the power of the referee to give his award in favor of the other man.

5. A man hanging on the ropes in a helpless state, with his toes off the ground, shall be

U.S. Military Boxing Manual

considered down.

6. No seconds or any other person to be allowed in the ring during the rounds.

7. Should the contest be stopped by any unavoidable interference, the referee to name the time and place as soon as possible for finishing the contest; so that the match must be won and lost, unless the backers of both men agree to draw the stakes.

8. The gloves to be fair-sized boxing gloves of the best quality and new.

U.S. Military Boxing Manual

9. Should a glove burst, or come off, it must be replaced to the referee's satisfaction.

10. A man on one knee is considered down and if struck is entitled to the stakes.

11. That no shoes or boots with spikes or springs be allowed.

12. The contest in all other respects to be governed by revised London Prize Ring Rules.

U.S. Military Boxing Manual

THE BOXER'S CODE

RULE I

Thou shalt never talk bad about any Rocky

movie. Thou shalt cry when Mickey passes.

RULE II

Thou shalt respect thy sparring partner. Thou

U.S. Military Boxing Manual

shalt spar at a speed that is neither slow nor fast, but at a tempo that provides a way for both boxers to learn, benefit, and gain experience from the sparring session.

RULE III

Thou shalt give a simple head nod or a tap of the glove to let your sparring partner know you are sorry for hitting them below the belt.

RULE IV

Thou shalt be courteous by asking your sparring partner "if they are okay" after landing a really good punch.

RULE V

Thou shalt respect the boxing gym by paying to

U.S. Military Boxing Manual

support its existence. Thou shalt encourage your friends, family, and anyone you come across to train Boxing by joining a Boxing Gym.

RULE VI

Thou shalt accept that Boxing Is The Mother Of All Martial Arts.

RULE VII

Thou shalt train boxing everyday. Thou shalt do conditioning and roadwork (running). Thou shalt train with the heavy bag, focus mitts, speed bag, and sparring with a trained boxer.

RULE VIII

Thou shalt support other boxers, boxing promoters, and the boxing industry in general

U.S. Military Boxing Manual

by promoting the benefits of the sport of Boxing

to friends, family, and strangers.

RULE IX

Thou shalt publicly praise the skills, charisma,

and the importance of boxing champions.

RULE X

Thou shalt always act in a sportsmanlike

manner towards other boxers and everyone

else thou come across.

The Darker Side of Boxing

Boxing was not always so clean-cut,

safe, and family-friendly as it is in the 21st

Century. Up until the wide spread adoption of

the Marquess of Queensberry Rules (1867),

U.S. Military Boxing Manual

boxing was dangerous, violent, and many times resulted in the death of its participants. Not only did the boxers punch, head-butt, bite, tear each other's skin, gouge, and pull each other's hair, but they also grappled. This was bare-knuckle boxing and it was the sport of boxing at its worst. This caused critics of boxing to label boxing as a dangerous sport. The boxers wrestled while standing in the clinch and many of the older boxing manuals in the 1800's like "Boxing Made Easy" (1865) featured and extolled specific standing grappling techniques. Spectators to a boxing match up until the late 18th century, could even witness boxing on the ground as well as standing. The adoption of the London Prize Ring Rules changed this in 1838 by stating that

U.S. Military Boxing Manual

a boxer knocked down had 30 seconds to stand with an additional 8 seconds to prepare himself to start again. In addition, holds and throws were allowed. With the adoption of codified rules governing the sport and providing more rules for the safety of boxers (standard gloves, etc), the sport grew in popularity over the past few hundred years to become the world's most popular family friendly combat sport.

Benefits of Boxing

• Reduced risk of heart disease, high blood pressure, colon cancer and diabetes
• Prevention of bone loss associated with aging, and a lower risk of osteoporosis
• Lower cholesterol levels

U.S. Military Boxing Manual

- Lower blood pressure and risk of stroke

- Stronger heart and lungs

- Healthier joints

- Increased muscle strength

- More success at keeping weight off

- Less body fat

- Better muscle tone

- Improved posture

- Improved sense of well-being

- Less depression

- More energy and stamina

- Increased productivity

- Better sleep

- Less stress and anxiety

- Better mobility and self-confidence

- Improved immunity to minor illnesses

U.S. Military Boxing Manual

Boxing as Diplomacy

In 19th Century Europe, Boxing was envisioned by some forward thinkers as a tool to stop war between two nations. If boxers could solve the diplomatic conflicts that nations endured in a honorable manner by representing their respective nations in the ring, nations would not have to dispatch armies to decimate each other on the field of battle. In the 19th century U.S., Boxing matches were organized by local political bosses. Because these political bosses "controlled" a district or area, they were able to host Boxing matches without being under threat from the authorities. According to legendary Boxer Mike Tyson, the red and the blue that is used in the Boxing ring and on Boxing gloves represented the

U.S. Military Boxing Manual

Democratic and Republican parties in the United States. Because political bosses were constantly vying for political power in order to increase their standing in their own political party and to increase the income generated by their political party, they would host boxing matches to decide the fate of a certain district. The district would be politically decided through the champions (top boxers) of each party boxing, represented in the ring by their recognized colors. The winning party would either retain or gain a new district and the losing party would relinquish their district to the winner.

U.S. Military Boxing Manual

Character

"Boxing is a contest of character and ingenuity. The boxer with more will, determination, desire, and intelligence is always the one who comes out the victor."

- Cus D'Amato

The handstand is effective for building core strength.

U.S. Military Boxing Manual

Boxing Still Number One

Boxers are the most skilled fighters in the world. It takes years of hard work to make a boxer. Anyone that has watched any one of the reality television shows on MMA has witnessed an MMA fighter created in a few months. The skills of a boxer take many years to master. It just looks like punching doesn't it? Sure, that is what boxing is to the novice. Boxing is an encyclopedia of which many individuals have read just one page and seem to feel they know it now. That is like reading a page from a book on heart surgery and deciding that you have learned it now. The tactics, strategies, nuances in the application of techniques, attention to minutiae, stamina, and fitness of boxers are unrivaled and

U.S. Military Boxing Manual

unparalleled by any MMA fighter. There are
over 50 million boxing fans in the United States
alone making it indisputably the most popular
combat sport in the United States of America.
This fact being indisputable is beyond
discussion. Throughout the world, Boxing is
immensely more popular even than it is in
America. On top of that, boxing fans are more
educated than MMA fans, with boxing fans
holding substantially more Graduate and Post-
Graduate university degrees. Most importantly,
women prefer boxing over MMA.

Treadmill vs Roadwork

Running on a treadmill is not roadwork.
The term "roadwork" in boxing terminology
indicates running outdoors. That is what all the

U.S. Military Boxing Manual

old manuals of boxing stipulate and there are many current boxing champions like Manny Pacquiao and Floyd Mayweather Jr. that swear by it. Why do some modern boxers run indoors? Because of lack of space, some professional boxers prefer to run indoors. But is this helping them or hurting them? It can be argued that it is neither hurting them nor helping them, but it is not assisting them reach their full potential in training.

Running outdoors has many advantages that running on a smooth surface does not. The changes in elevation, grade changes, inclines, declines, and obstacles assist the boxer in their cardio, stamina, endurance, breath control, and their balance. Boxers that run outdoors use their hamstrings more than on a treadmill and

U.S. Military Boxing Manual

the hamstrings are among the most important

muscles for generating punching power.

Boxers that run outdoors experience wind

resistance and this too assists them train

harder. Running outdoors also increases a

boxer's eye-foot coordination and makes the

U.S. Military Boxing Manual

boxer stay alert as to the incoming obstacles or

objects in his or her direction. An unfocused

U.S. Military Boxing Manual

boxer running outdoors could result in injuries

and this raises the boxer's observational

awareness. Professional boxers should make

an effort to run outdoors on a regular basis as

its advantages far outweigh running on a

treadmill.

The Job of a Boxing Coach

The prime responsibility of a boxing

coach is that he is absolutely sure that each of

his men is physically sound and able to

participate in boxing without fear of

endangering his physical well-being.

Secondly, he is responsible to see that he does

everything possible to get his men in as good

a physical condition as possible. In order to

function safely and effectively in boxing, it is

U.S. Military Boxing Manual

imperative that a man is in top physical shape.

The road to good physical condition for boxing

is not an easy one. The average person,

especially an inexperienced one, is not capable

of working himself hard enough to obtain the

level of condition he needs. A coach must be

able to demand and get that work from his

charges.

U.S. Military Boxing Manual

Well Directed Blow

"Travelers should be well versed in Boxing. It is a consolation to a man in a strange country, that he is equal to repel any attack made by another in a natural way, and sometimes to entertain the hopes of proving victorious over numbers (of men). Nay in cafes where the sword and pistol are used, a timely and well directed blow will revenge the pugilist on his enemy or defeat the villainous attempt."

- Thomas Fewtrell. Boxing Reviewed (1790)

The Boxing Shoe

From the 18th century till the early 20th century, boxing was done wearing boots, dress shoes, or whatever else they could find to wear. Although this had to do more with

U.S. Military Boxing Manual

fashion or reasons of necessity, rather than as a specifically chosen item by boxers. The boot, for example, provided good traction but allowed for poor mobility. With the creation of the modern boxing shoe, boxers would become faster, have better mobility, and be able to maneuver in ways that their previous shoes had prevented.

The modern boxing shoe was invented by Everlast through a partnership between sporting goods store owner Jacob Golomb (a tailor's son) and Jack Dempsey in 1916. Dempsey introduced Golomb to Boxing and commissioned custom leather boxing shoes to be made for him. This was the start of the Everlast brand and its rise to international

U.S. Military Boxing Manual

popularity. These leather boxing shoes were to be light, generate traction to prevent slipping, had rubber soles, and provided sufficient ankle support. Some modern boxing shoes manufacturers include Adidas, Title, and even Nike through partnership with Michael Jordan. Boxing shoes allow the constant footwork and fast mobility that a boxer needs to avoid punches and to strike with a solid base. Without them, boxers would not be able to maneuver as quickly as they do or strike with as much power.

Undefeated Boxers

They have never lost. Losing implies that the individual that lost made mistakes that contributed to their loss (meaning they have

U.S. Military Boxing Manual

not yet mastered their craft) or the individual that won possessed greater skills, sparred more rounds or possessed greater stamina. In many situations, an undefeated boxer may even lose by judges decision. But an undefeated boxer like Floyd Mayweather Jr. is undefeated because he has mastered his craft meaning that he has mastered the art of boxing. His opponents are now younger than him, less experienced and this puts them at a disadvantage. The advantage in the art of boxing goes to the individual that has completely mastered offensive and defensive maneuvers. To paraphrase legendary Boxing trainer Cus D'Amato, "The win goes to the person that sparred more rounds and ran further. Destiny owes that person the victory." Joe Calzaghe Jr., an undefeated and retired boxer with a record of 46-0 achieved this by mastering his craft. It is by mastery of the art of boxing that their opponents lose. Why is this? This is because Mayweather Jr. and Calzaghe made all the mistakes they needed

U.S. Military Boxing Manual

to as an amateur and in their first fights, but as they progressed and rose their mastery of the art of boxing became evident for all to witness. Their defensive skills are exemplary. Their ability to dodge, evade, bob, weave, block, feint and counter repeatedly under pressure exemplify their mastery. The worst and most un-generous comment anyone could make is to say that undefeated boxers like Mayweather and Calzaghe fought opponents that were not important. Was legendary boxer Oscar De La Hoya important when Mayweather defeated him? Of course. Were legendary boxers Bernard Hopkins and Roy Jones Jr. important when Calzaghe defeated them? Of course. If a boxer is too old to fight, they should not get in to the ring. George Foreman was 45 years old

when he re-gained the Heavyweight

championship belt, so age is not an issue.

Undefeated boxers are legends and they

should be honored for their excellence.

U.S. Military Boxing Manual

Hand Wrapping

Be sure that each of your boxers knows how and correctly wraps his hands before each workout. The reason for wrapping hands is principally to protect the bones in the back of the hand. The wrap should be put on snugly but should not bind the hand. The most important part of the wrap is the crosses over the back of the hand. On a properly wrapped hand, the bandage will stay in place even after gloves have been changed during the workout. Be sure to check your boxers' wraps every few days. The activities that should be included in a workout program are running, shadow boxing, sparring, rope skipping, heavy bag and calisthenics.

U.S. Military Boxing Manual

The Boxing Glove

The boxing glove was invented by bare knuckle boxing champion John "Jack" Broughton (1703-1798). Jack Broughton created "mufflers" that were used for sparring. Broughton had opened an arena on Tottenham Court Road in London, England. The arena featured various types of fight events including man versus bear and weapon fighting. The padding in Broughton's gloves is what differentiated the "muffler" and the Roman "cestus". Although the Roman "cestus" was an ancient type of glove, it really consisted of leather wraps with protruding studded metal pieces attached. Broughton's "muffler" was uniquely different and its ability to reduce the impact of blows was readily apparent. The first

40

U.S. Military Boxing Manual

time Broughton's gloves were used in a boxing match was in Aix-la-Chapelle, France in 1818. After the adoption of the Marquess of Queensberry Rules, the gloves that were adopted weighed 2 ounces or less. It was the boxing match between John L Sullivan and James J Corbett that popularized the 5 ounce boxing glove as this match was the first gloved Heavyweight Championship of the world. For reasons of safety, the weight of the modern boxing glove has increased to 8 ounces and 10 ounces. The reason for this is to protect the fighters. Tampering with a boxing glove is a criminal offense and any trainer caught doing so would face definite jail time. In June 1983, boxer Luis Resto defeated Billy Collins Jr in Madison Square Garden in New York. Resto

U.S. Military Boxing Manual

was found by the New York State Boxing
Commission to have had at least ounce of
padding removed from each boxing glove.
Resto was criminally found guilty of criminal
possession of a weapon (Resto's hands),
assault, and conspiracy.

Roadwork

Running is the most indispensable
activity in the program. If time permitted only
one activity, running should be the one
selected. If should be done in a spring, jog,
walk fashion rather than a steady pace. In
boxing the pace is seldom steady, but one in
which there are periods of relative inactivity
and others of furious activity; hence, the
advisability of the change of pace in roadwork.

U.S. Military Boxing Manual

JACK BURKE

U.S. Military Boxing Manual

Tyson vs Spinks

On June 27th 1988, "Iron" Mike Tyson (34-0, 30 KO) defeated Michael Spinks (31-0, 21 KO) in Atlantic City, New Jersey to become the Undisputed Heavyweight Boxing Champion of the world. Mike Tyson was WBC, WBA, and IBF Heavyweight Champion but Michael Spinks was the Ring Magazine and the lineal Heavyweight Champion. Mike Tyson knocked out Michael Spinks after 91 seconds in the first round of the match. Tyson made approximately $20,000,000 for 91 seconds of work.

Shadow Boxing

If done properly shadow boxing is an excellent developer of good form and a good

U.S. Military Boxing Manual

conditioner. The men must be prodded to put out to the fullest the entire time he is Shadow boxing. Working in front of a mirror is excellent help toward developing good form.

Sparring

Sparring is very important, of course, but should not be continued for too long on a particular day. The usual length of a sparring session should be two or three rounds of the same duration as matches. Occasionally, the sessions may be extended to four rounds, but never more. There should always be a plan for a sparring session, something a man is to especially work out for that day; never spar just to be sparring. Be sure men wear headgear and grease their faces when sparring. Sparring is usually done early in the workout when men are fresh enough to try new skills and work on new combinations.

Six Weeks

The usual time allotted to training a man for a contested struggle is six weeks. The objects to be obtained in this time are:

1) The removal of superfluous fat and water

2) The increase of contractile power in the muscles

3) Increased endurance

4) Increased "Wind" or the power of breathing

- John Boyle O'Reilly, Ethics of Boxing and Manly Sport (1888)

U.S. Military Boxing Manual

Jumping Rope

Jumping rope is not a substitute for roadwork; it is more designed to improve coordination and agility. It should be done continuously and broken into period of fast and slow (i.e. 45 seconds easy, 15 seconds hard) times 5 minutes. It is especially valuable for those men who find it hard to learn to skip rope; they are the people who need the coordination and agility it develops.

U.S. Military Boxing Manual

Heavy Bag

The heavy bag is one of the most valuable pieces of equipment to use in your workouts. It not only helps develop power and improve form but also is an excellent conditioner. It may be punched while being held by a coach to work on a particular punch or combination of punches, or may be boxed as you would an opponent. When working on the heavy bag, one should hit bag when it is coming toward you, but has not yet reached the vertical position. The hands should be carefully wrapped when punching the heavy bag. The heavy bag should not be used during the last few days before a bout, since it does have a tendency to slow down arm speed. Coaches must carefully look at the boxers'

U.S. Military Boxing Manual

hands to ensure that they are not injuring their hands and knuckles due to excessive bag-work.

Calisthenics

The calisthenics to be stressed in boxing training are stomach work and neck work. Sit-ups or curls are the best stomach exercises for the upper abdominals, and leg raising exercises for the best for the lower abdominals. The best neck exercises are partner-resisted lateral and vertical neck flexions. Push-ups are an excellent way to improve punch strength. Calisthenics should be included in each day's workout. Coaches are encouraged to look at Coaching Olympic Style Boxing by the United States Olympic

U.S. Military Boxing Manual

Training Center for skills, drills, and example workouts.

TECHNIQUE VS BRUTE STRENGTH

"As I run over the past thirty-five years I can recall many a brawny bruiser making fierce splashes in the boxing world for a short while. And then along comes some dandy stylist, who dances all around the slugger, stabs him with all of the 57 varieties of annoying blows, laughs at his clumsy efforts, and carries off the decision and whatever glory goes with it. A bruiser never lasts long, a clever boxer always does."

- Boxing, Jack O'Brien (1878-1942)

U.S. Military Boxing Manual

Average Day's Workout

5 minutes of loosening up

2 rounds of shadow boxing.

2 rounds of sparring.

2 four rounds heavy bag.

2 rounds rope skipping.

Calisthenics.

Roadwork - 2 - 3 miles - (Spring - Jog - Walk)

Offense vs Defense

"Boxing as a sport is characterized by a

constant shift between attack and defense,

each being important and depending upon the

other for successful execution. Without attack

there is no necessity for defense, and without

defense there would be no attack. That a

strong offense is supposedly the best defense

U.S. Military Boxing Manual

is in general true, especially if defensive skill is the foundation of attack. Without underlying defensive strength there always comes a time when a good attack meets a better one."

- Edwin Haislet, Boxing (1940)

Training Tips

1. Always wrap hands carefully.

2. Loosen up well before and after workouts.

3. Do not work to the point of excessive fatigue.

4. Make workouts short and spirited.

5. Work according to timed rounds.

U.S. Military Boxing Manual

6. About 10-12 rounds of work is sufficient.

7. Spar with a purpose - not just to be working.

8. Supervise sparring closely.

9. Use large gloves for sparring (16 oz.)

10. Include stomach exercises in every workout.

11. Shadow box for form - think while shadow boxing.

12. Do not sit down during workout - keep moving.

U.S. Military Boxing Manual

13. Wear headgear while sparring.

14. Use grease on face during sparring drills.

15. On heavy bag wear bag gloves and work on series punching.

16. Do not lose weight unnaturally to box in a lower weight.

17. Avoid excessive drying out.

18. Do not use the "sweat box."

19. Do roadwork frequently- use intervals and fartlek-style runs.

U.S. Military Boxing Manual

20. If you have time for just one thing in a workout - run.

21. Keep regular habits of sleeping, eating, and exercising.

22. Never disregard any injury - no matter how slight.

23. Keep all workout clothing clean and sanitary.

24. Spar with smaller men for speed - spar with bigger men for power (no more than two weight-class difference).

25. Stay relaxed at all times.

U.S. Military Boxing Manual

Cicero

"It is exercise alone that supports the spirits and keeps the mind in vigor."

- Cicero (106 B.C.E.-43 B.C.E.)

INCREASING PUNCH SPEED

The punch of a trained professional boxer can reach up to 500 kilograms of force. What is a punch? A punch is a whip-like motion of the arm with the purpose of striking. According to Oxford Dictionary, the word "punch" was a Middle English variant of the word "pounce" (noun), which means "a sudden swoop or spring". It described the motion carried out by a person that is either stamping or punching an object.

U.S. Military Boxing Manual

How is the force of the punch generated?

Potential energy travels from the ground up to

the legs of the boxer and is transferred from

each muscle in sequential order until the

potential energy reaches the arm of the boxer.

The sequential "firing" of each muscle involved

in the punch ensures that the potential energy

builds up before being released in the form of

kinetic energy. The potential energy becomes

kinetic energy after it is released by the motion

of the punch. The main muscles that are used

in punching are the gastrocnemius (calf

muscle), rectus femoris (front thigh muscle,

part of the quadriceps), and biceps femoris

(back thigh muscle, part of hamstrings). The

arm generates less than 5% of the punch's

power. The arm is used to deliver the kinetic

U.S. Military Boxing Manual

energy. The analogy would be a bullet to a gun. The boxer's arm is the gun and the punch is the bullet. Kinetic energy equals mass multiplied by the velocity squared. So a larger arm should generate more power but mass alone without adequate velocity would not yield the proper result. Many bodybuilders have ripped and damaged their arms attempting to throw punches without proper training and technique. This is why lifting weights is not necessarily creating more punching power. In other words, a heavier arm is a slower arm or a lighter arm is a faster (higher velocity) arm. In addition, the punching technique of the boxer would have to be efficient and proper in order to generate the necessary velocity required.

U.S. Military Boxing Manual

As any boxing trainer would attest to, a boxer with sloppy technique can never generate the amount of force of a boxer with proper technique. An arm puncher or a puncher that relies on their arm strength to deliver punches would be at a great disadvantage in contrast to a boxer that uses their body to properly generate force for their punch. The solid (static) base stance by the boxer, shifting of their weight, and pivoting are important for the transfer of potential energy in sequential order from the ground up to the ankles, knees, thighs, core (abdomen), chest, shoulders, and to the punching arm where it is released as kinetic energy. In order to increase your punching power, you would have to focus on exercises that strengthen your calf muscles,

U.S. Military Boxing Manual

front and back thigh muscles, core, chest,

shoulders, and arms. The body has to work

together in sequence to generate punching

force and that is why your training should also

be well-rounded.

Key Points In Boxing

1. Stance.

a. Relaxed.

b. Feet spread to side as well as back and

forth.

c. Knees flexed slightly.

e. Hips and shoulders parallel to the ground.

U.S. Military Boxing Manual

f. Body bent forward slightly at waist

g. Non-dominant hip and shoulder forward.

h. Chin down on breast bone.

i. Look out of top of eyes.

j. Lead hand held high, level with your eye.

k. Rear hand held in, level with chin.

l. Elbows held in to the sides.

2. Footwork

a. Move foot closest to the direction in which you want to move first.

U.S. Military Boxing Manual

b. Shuffle rather than jump.

c. Circle away from your opponent's power, or rear hand.

d. Work on moving in and out constantly.

e. A moving target is not easily hit.

f. Move in every time you punch.

g. Never cross feet.

h. Feet never closer together than they are when you take stance.

U.S. Military Boxing Manual

3. Jab.

a. Speed and form are the most important considerations.

b. Complete extension of arm; elbow in—like a hinge.

c. Twist of body-pivot.

d. Palm down.

e. Step simultaneously with extension of arm.

f. Fist doubled up tight.

g. A definite blow - not a flick.

U.S. Military Boxing Manual

h. Rear hand held in; don't drop your hand.

i. Most important blow.

j. Bring back to position quickly.

4. Defense for jab.

The first defense for all blows is a good, tight on-guard stance!!

a. Block right hand blows with left hand and left hand blows with right.

Defensive for jab, Jab "Catch" - as jab is coming toward face, simply open corresponding hand and catch the blow a very short distance from face.

U.S. Military Boxing Manual

(1) Move into the blow slightly to keep it from pushing back into your face.

(2) Do not alter the stance by bringing your shoulder out.

(3) Block inside the left hand.

c. Parry - as blow approached the face, corresponding hand opens and flicks the oncoming blow to the inside with a wrist motion.

(1) Do not alter stance.

(2) Block very close to face do not reach for blow.

U.S. Military Boxing Manual

5. Cross.

a. Complete pivot of body first.

b. Hand stays in front of shoulder until it lands.

c. Palm down.

d. Punch through the target - not just to it.

e. Usually most effective after a jab lead.

f. Power is based in hip and shoulder.

g. Lead hand (jab hand) comes back to face for protection; don't drop hands!!

U.S. Military Boxing Manual

6. Defense for cross.

a. Inside parry easiest defense.

(1) Same as for the jab—same side defense: his left w/ your right; his right with your left.

(2) Keep other hand up to defend against follow-on blows or to counter-punch with.

7. Hook

a. Most difficult blow to throw correctly.

b. A close range blow.

c. Usually most effective in series.

d. Arm remains bent throughout the blow.

U.S. Military Boxing Manual

e. Palm is held outwards or down.

f. Arm is whipped in an arc around body.

g. Shoulder slightly precedes the arm around.

h. Weight transfers to rear leg.

i. Other hand held high to protect face.

j. Avoid locking the "hooking" arm; remember, it is a bent-arm punch.

l. Be sure straight punches are mastered before hook is attempted!

m. At this level, you can win by throwing straight, crisp punches.

8. Defense for Hook

a. Step in to the punch and "smother" it by getting close to your opponent. Step into the punch, and let it fall harmlessly over your shoulders.

b. Bob and weave.

(1) Slip the punch by bending the knees and rolling with the punch. Continue to duck, and allow the punch to travel over your head.

(2) Once you have "Ducked" the punch, reverse the direction of the "bob," weave back

U.S. Military Boxing Manual

into an upright position and immediately

counter to your opponent's open side.

Body Blows

9. Straight Jab to the Body.

a. Not a damaging blow.

b. Best used to open up an opponent.

c. Bend at the knees, not at the waist.

d. Punch is thrown straight out from the

shoulder.

10. Cross to the Body.

a. Very damaging counter for the left lead.

U.S. Military Boxing Manual

b. Excellent weapon against a "jabber".

c. Easy blow to learn.

d. Throw just like a cross to the head, but drop down to the body level.

e. Keep lead hand high.

f. Step forward.

g. Drive blow under the heart.

h. Keep hand in front of shoulder.

U.S. Military Boxing Manual

11. Hook to Body.

a. Dangerous blow to deliver.

b. Unwise to teach to novices.

c. Force of the blow should be across and up.

d. Excellent and damaging counter for the advanced boxer against an opposite-handed opponent's jab.

e. Extreme care must be taken not to telegraph the blow.

U.S. Military Boxing Manual

12. Defense for Body Blows

a. Elbow Block.

(1) Bring right elbow in front of left hand blows and vice versa for right hand blows.

(2) Keep elbow in against body.

(3) Keep opposite hand in position.

b. "Brush away" - best defense for body blows.

(1) Use right to block lefts and vice versa.

(2) Keep elbow in place and drop hand down over an oncoming blow.

(3) Blow is knocked down and out.

U.S. Military Boxing Manual

(4) Oncoming blow may be deflected anywhere on the forearm

(5) Use open hand for all blocking.

13. General Rules for Punching.

a. Snap punches, do not push them.

b. Punch through your target, not just to it.

c. Return your hands to their original position after throwing a blow.

d. Step in each time you punch.

e. Straight blows will ordinarily beat hooks to the punch.

U.S. Military Boxing Manual

f. Concentrate on straight punches until you have them mastered before going on to hooks.

g. As one hand lands, other hand must be on your chin.

14. General Rules for Defense.

a. Block as close to you as possible.

b. Use open hand to increase blocking surface.

c. Meet force with force.

d. Do not reach for punches.

e. Make blocking incidental - do not take a blocking stance.

U.S. Military Boxing Manual

15. Combinations

Some combination blows: Jab=1, Cross=2,

Lead-hand hook=3, Rear-hand uppercut=4,

Lead-hand uppercut=5.

a. 1-1, 1-1-1

b. 1-2-1, 1-1-2-1,

c. 1-2-3, 1-2-3-2-1

d. 1-2-3-4-1, 1-2-3-4-5-2-1

PREPARATION FOR BOUTS

In preparing your boxers for a coming

bout, be sure to get your men in the best

physical condition, but cut down on their

strenuous work about two days before the

bout. Two days before the bout, they should

work about 8 - 10 fast rounds with no heavy

sparring or heavy bag punching. The day

U.S. Military Boxing Manual

before the bout very little or loosening up type workout may be used, or no work at all need be done. You should try to find out as much as you can about the opponents your men are about to meet, and try to work on special techniques or plans of attack that might prove especially effective against the coming opponents. Your discussion of opponents with your men should tend to inspire confidence and not unduly alarm them. Pre-fight food consumption should be limited to carbohydrates and liquids. Avoid greasy and fatty foods as they slow digestion. Ordinarily, a meal is completely digested and out of the stomach in four hours, but the usual tension before a bout tends to slow down this process, so the pre-bout meal should not be overly

U.S. Military Boxing Manual

large. Foregoing the noon meal would not be a good idea because there may be some weakness if a man were to go all day without food. It is a very important part a good coach's job to see that his men are psychologically set for their bouts. This job is one that must be adapted to each individual's particular makeup. A coach must do all he can to learn his boxers' makeup and approach that will most effectively help then to best realize their potential. Some men will need to be pushed hard and others need to be deflated a little to combat overconfidence or complacency. It is up to the coach to determine which approach is called for with a particular man. Get to know your men as well as you can.

U.S. Military Boxing Manual

THE BOUT

On the afternoon of the bout there is a definite routine that a coach should set up for his boxers.

1. Be sure your boxers are present in the gym well before the scheduled time of the bouts.

2. Have men obtain their equipment, and be sure of correct fit.

3. Have men dress and be sure that their hands are correctly wrapped. (It is a good idea for the coach to wrap their hands.)

4. Put on gloves and adjust the headgear for correct fit. Be sure he has his mouthpiece.

U.S. Military Boxing Manual

5. Apply a coating of grease to the face, particularly the nose, lips, cheekbones and over the eyes.

6. Have the men warm up well at least two rounds. If the boxer is boxing after the first bout, have him begin his warm-up at the beginning of the bout before his.

7. Have the boxer immediately outside his corner when the bout before him ends.

8. Have the boxer enter the ring as soon as the corner is free.

9. Make a last minute check of his equipment and put his mouthpiece in place.

U.S. Military Boxing Manual

10. Give a last word of encouragement or advice.

BETWEEN ROUNDS

Seconding

The prime reason for seconds is to refresh the boxer between rounds. He should feel better after the rest period than before. The routine that should be followed is:

1. Have a stool ready for him when he returns to the corner.

2. Have him sit erect with his feet flat on the floor and his lower leg at a 90-degree angle from the floor. His hands should be on his lap.

U.S. Military Boxing Manual

3. Take the mouthpiece from and put water over it to clean it off.

4. Have him take about three deeps breaths to more or less slow him down, since he will be quite excited when he sits down. If will assist him in relaxing.

5. Clean off his face with a damp towel, but be sure to wipe it dry again.

6. Replace a coating of Vaseline over his face.

7. Give your boxer three things to work on; anything else he'll most likely not remember. Remember, your boxer will be "hyped up;" your job is to calm him down and help him

U.S. Military Boxing Manual

win!

8. At the ten second replace the mouthpiece.

9. Remove the stool at the bell and help lift your boxer from the stool. The routine of seconding should be practiced beforehand. Not more than two men should be used. One man's job should be taking care of the mouthpiece, towel and the grease. The second man should be used to handle the stool, water bucket, etc.

COACHING BETWEEN ROUNDS

A man cannot be taught to box in the one minute rest period. The best a coach can hope to accomplish during this brief interval is

U.S. Military Boxing Manual

to help this man to recall and perform skills he has previously learned. One man should do the talking between rounds. He should stress one or two items that will help to improve the boxer's performance, and he should repeat the advice two or three times in order to get it across to his man, the last time just as the bell rings.

BOUT STRATEGY

Be prepared to box at full speed for the entire three rounds. Be warmed up well, start fast, and try to get in the first punch.

Against Sluggers

1. Rely principally on straight punches.

2. Move constantly.

U.S. Military Boxing Manual

3. Attack suddenly.

4. Don't slug with him.

Against a Jabber or Tall Opponent

1. Move inside the jab.

2. Once inside keep punching.

3. Make extensive use of the right hook over the jab and the straight right to the body.

4. Keep pressure on him.

Against an Opposite-Handed Opponent

1. Move away from his rear, or power, hand.

U.S. Military Boxing Manual

2. Best weapon is a cross.

3. Do not fight his way - if he wants you to lead, wait; if he wants to lead, go to him.

4. A lead-hand hook may be a good weapon, but a jab is generally of not much value, use a double jab.

5. Keep your lead high nullify his jab hand.

U.S. Military Boxing Manual

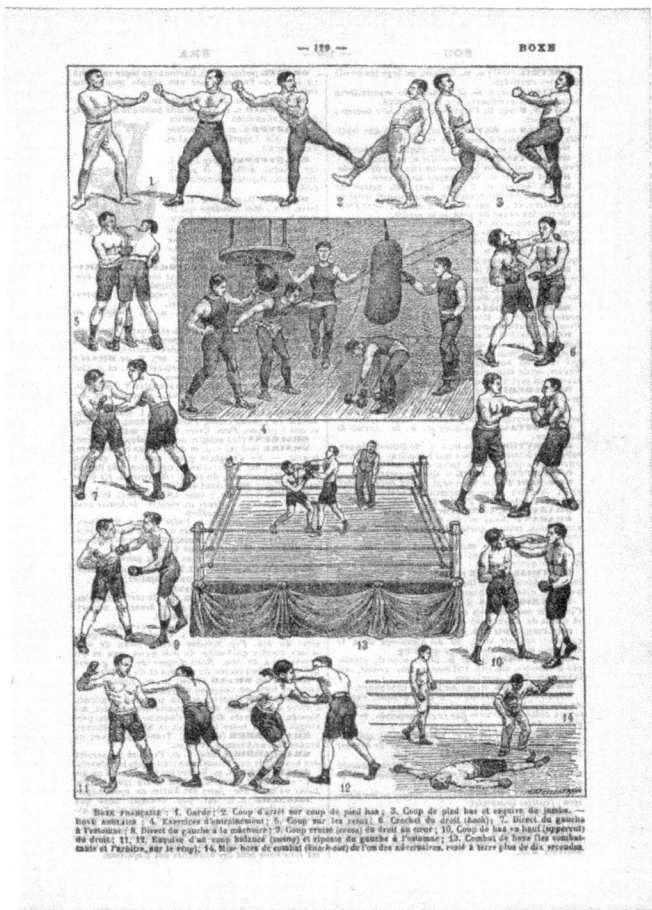

Against a counter-puncher

1. Do not lead with single punches.

U.S. Military Boxing Manual

2. Try to make him lead.

3. Punch in series and then get out.

4. Attack suddenly.

Against a man who boxes from a crouch

1. He'll probably throw mostly hooks.

2. Move constantly.

3. Step in with straight one-twos.

4. Hold your hands relatively wide apart.

U.S. Military Boxing Manual

Nature of the Activity

Boxing covers all aspects of amateur boxing and exposes students to situations in which fear and perceived dangers are present. Stance, movement, basic punches (jab, cross, hook, and upper cut), defenses, strategy, and tactics are taught.

Purpose of the Warning

The purpose of the following information is to inform the boxer of the risk of potential injury in boxing. Information, regarding proper conditioning, healthful hints, and safety are shared in hopes of creating a more productive experience. Describing all potential injuries that a boxer may sustain while participating in boxing is not conceivable, but utilizing the

U.S. Military Boxing Manual

proper execution of fundamentals, elements of instruction, and care of equipment remains imperative for the safety and zest of those participating.

Potential Injuries

The following list represents potential injuries that may occur in boxing:

1. Boxers may experience head injuries which including: concussion, malocclusions, fractures, and broken noses.

2. Boxers may severely stretch or tear muscles and tendons in the legs, arms, back, ankles, and wrists

U.S. Military Boxing Manual

3. Boxers may develop blisters and sores on the feet that later may lead to infection if the correct shoes are not worn.

4. Boxers may amass injury to the mouth and teeth if mouthpieces are not worn.

5. Boxers may be injured if the gym floor is not void of dirt, gravel, and wet spots.

Conditioning

1. The individual boxer should work on flexibility, strength, and endurance daily.

2. Stretching activities for the individual should precede all boxing classes for joint flexibility

U.S. Military Boxing Manual

and muscular elasticity. Time is not allotted in class for stretching so the boxer should stretch prior to arriving.

3. Boxers should be aware that the idea of conditioning is a continuous process. The boxing course is designed to teach specific skills not get the boxer "in shape". The boxer has the responsibility to ensure that he is appropriately conditioned.

4. Boxers should appreciate that the well-conditioned athlete will perform with fewer injuries. The more you sweat in training the less you bleed in the ring.

U.S. Military Boxing Manual

Health Tips

1. Proper warm-up will be of help in reducing muscle soreness.

2. Boxers should inform the instructor of any disability or illness and report any and all injuries.

3. Communication should be strong between all members of the team. Boxers must employ the buddy team method of monitoring each other's well-being.

4. Boxers should remember that proper diet and rest is directly related to top performances.

U.S. Military Boxing Manual

Safety

Boxing is a contact combative sport which is governed by a set of strict rules. Even when the rules are strictly adhered to, the possibility of injury is present. Should you encounter any physical problems or impairments prior to class or during the course of a class, you must immediately notify the instructor. As previously stated, no amount of instruction, precaution, and supervision will totally eliminate all risk of serious, catastrophic, or even fatal injury. You must accept a degree of responsibility for managing the risks inherent in boxing in order to get the most out of the experience.

U.S. Military Boxing Manual

Boxing Quiz

1) Who won the first Heavyweight Boxing championship? (Post-Queensberry)

2) Which retired, undefeated boxer holds a 46-0 record and was recently inducted in to the International Boxing Hall of Fame?

3) Who invented the boxing glove?

4) Which boxer inspired the invention of the boxing shoe?

5) Name the boxing trainer for Brandon Rios and Marcos Maidana.

6) Name the boxing trainer for Manny

U.S. Military Boxing Manual

Pacquiao and Miguel Cotto.

7) Who won the longest boxing match in history (Pre-Queensberry)?

8) Who is the only retired undefeated Heavyweight Champion of the world?

9) Who was the oldest Heavyweight Champion of the world?

10) Who was the youngest Heavyweight Champion of the world?

11) Who was the fattest boxer in history?

12) What is the main responsibility of a boxing

U.S. Military Boxing Manual

trainer?

13) Who was the first English Bare Knuckle Boxing Champion?

14) Who was the first African-American Heavyweight Boxing Champion?

15) Who is the only boxer to win the Heavyweight Championship 3 times?

16) Which boxer holds the Guinness World Record for the Most Contact Punches in a Minute?

17) Name Mike Tyson's trainer and legal guardian.

U.S. Military Boxing Manual

18) Name Muhammad Ali's and Sugar Ray Leonard's trainer.

19) How large approximately is a professional boxing ring? (In feet)

20) What is the world's fastest knockout? (In seconds)

KEY

1) John L Sullivan 2) Joe Calzaghe 3) John "Jack" Broughton 4) Jack Dempsey 5) Robert Garcia 6) Freddie Roach 7) Jack Burke 8) Rocky Marciano 9) George Foreman 10) Mike Tyson 11) Eric Esch aka "Butterbean" 12) Fight Preparation 13) James Figg 14) Jack Johnson 15) Muhammad Ali 16) Keith Lidell 17) Cus

U.S. Military Boxing Manual

D'Amato 18) Angelo Dundee 19) 16-24 Feet

20) 4 seconds

BOXING RECORDS

FASTEST KNOCKOUT

Where: Minneapolis, Minnesota

When: November 4th, 1947

Who: Mike Collins (W) vs. Pat Brownson (L)

Time: 4 Seconds after the bell

Source: Guinness World Records

U.S. Military Boxing Manual

Kambiz Mostofizadeh Conditioning Program

    a. 100 Push-Ups or 100 Burpees

    b. 3 x 60 Seconds Running In Place

    c. 100 Jumping Jacks

    d. 100 180 Degree Jumping Spins

    e. 100 Airplane II Movements

    f. 100 Wall Push-Ups

    g. 2 x 60 Seconds Wall Handstand

    h. 10 Rounds x 60 Punches = 600 Punches

    i. 3 x 3 Minutes Heavy Bag

U.S. Military Boxing Manual

MIKAZUKI PUBLISHING HOUSE CATALOGUE
Mikazuki Jujitsu Manual
25 Principles of Martial Arts
Karate 360
Political Advertising Manual
Learning Magic
Stories of a Street Performer (Pop Haydn)
Magic as Science & Religion
The Bribe Vibe
World War Water
Small Arms & Deep Pockets
Arctic Black Gold
Find the Ideal Husband
John Locke's 2nd Treatise on Civil Government
The History of Acid Tripping
I Dream In Haiku
Mikazuki Political Science Manual
Tokiwa; A Japanese Love Story
The Card Party; Theater Play
Hagakure; The Book of Hidden Leaves
MMA Coloring Book
DIY Comic Book
Freakshow Los Angeles
Swords & Sails: The Legacy of the Red Lion
Coming to America Handbook
The Medium Writer
California's Next Century 2.0: Economic Renaissance
Self-Examination Diary: Good and Bad Deeds Log
Master Password Organizer Handbook
George Washington's Farewell Address
Customer Profile Organizer
United Nations Charter
DIY Comic Book Part II
Storyboard Book: Make Your Movie Series
Basketball Team Play Design Book
Football Play Design Book
T-Shirt Design Book
Rappers Rhyme Book: Lyricists Notebook
Japan History Coloring Book

U.S. Military Boxing Manual

Magicians Coloring Book
The Adventures of Sherlock Holmes
Words of King Darius
The Art of War
The Book of Five Rings
Tao Te Ching
Captain Bligh's Voyage
Beginner's Magician Manual
The Man that Made the English Language
The Arrival of Palloncino
The Irish Republican Army Manual of Guerrilla Warfare
Living the Pirate Code
Van Carlton Detective Agency; The Burgundy Diamond
Quotes Gone Wild
Shogun X the Last Immortal
The Art of Western Boxing
William Shakespeare's Sonnets
U.S. Military Boxing Manual

Education Is the Key to Happiness

U.S. Military Boxing Manual

NOTES

U.S. Military Boxing Manual

NOTES

U.S. Military Boxing Manual

NOTES

U.S. Military Boxing Manual

NOTES

U.S. Military Boxing Manual

NOTES

U.S. Military Boxing Manual

NOTES

U.S. Military Boxing Manual

NOTES

U.S. Military Boxing Manual

NOTES

U.S. Military Boxing Manual

NOTES

U.S. Military Boxing Manual

NOTES

NOTES

U.S. Military Boxing Manual

NOTES

U.S. Military Boxing Manual

NOTES

U.S. Military Boxing Manual

NOTES

U.S. Military Boxing Manual

NOTES

U.S. Military Boxing Manual

NOTES

U.S. Military Boxing Manual

NOTES

U.S. Military Boxing Manual

NOTES

U.S. Military Boxing Manual

NOTES

U.S. Military Boxing Manual

NOTES

U.S. Military Boxing Manual

NOTES

U.S. Military Boxing Manual

NOTES

NOTES

www.ingramcontent.com/pod-product-compliance
Lightning Source LLC
Chambersburg PA
CBHW071559040426
42452CB00008B/1222